# To Speak of Grasses

# To Speak of Grasses

ISBN 9781763825901

Cover image taken in Karijini National Park,
Western Australia, by the author.

Walleah Press
South Launceston
Tasmania, Australia 7249

www.walleahpress.com.au
ralph.wessman@walleahpress.com.au

**Walleah Press**

# To Speak of Grasses

Kathryn Fry

# Contents

*For Macy, Lyla, Etta and June*

# Suspended

**Forecast**


Lotus buds tight as the tips of tulips emerge
        slowly, one after the other over summer

each rising above the leafy greenery
        as flags raising hope for the Earth.

They swell over days into deep pink
        double rows of petals, their flamboyance

a bright play dulling fear for a while.
        The sacred lotus at home in the exotic tropics

thrives in our newly humid heat.
        To be trawled by bees, tossed by wind

to bear fruit with seeds housed in cells
        like monks in their temple, meditating

as they must through the hours.
        This sacred lotus, its leaves open for alms.

And when we watered the world
        of our earthen pot, drops rolled

over the pads and spiralled into their centres.
        Every morning, we would look for blooms

in the labyrinth of stems, a ritual like scrolling
        for the forecast, for news of flood or fire.

**Revelations from Dudley**


A ribbon of morning-lit glitter reaches the rocks
                  through the sweep of sea from the horizon
out near the edge of the Sydney Basin. That hole

into which all manner of debris fell
                  after the Great Dying. I recall a vista of blue
from the jagged peak of Mt Tomaree, finding islands

in the sun, a Gould's petrel flying
                  below, and that rush of feeling, though you
weren't there. Sandstone I'm sitting on now

is two-fifty-two million years old, so I'm learning
                  from a geologist on the move, his arms wide
with the verve of this ancient story: of river energies

flood plains and sediment brought down.
                  Images of swamped land inundated our screens
of water draining south, no longer to forests

of *Glossopteris*, that Gondwanan seed-bearer.
                  Now I know it took ten thousand years
to form one metre of coal, the dark driver of change.

He's showing the group pumice from the under-sea
                  explosion only a dozen years ago.
And he's reading an overhang like a book he learned

by heart. I think of you, our different ways
            as he points to cross-beds and current flow, bands
of varied sizes, and aquifer water under pressure.

We're soon to find iron-rich fossilised trunks
            lying willy-nilly, but I'm stuck on tension
between plates or any-two-things close

like you and me, and the stresses of our years:
            scant stuff on the earth's clock yet, here we are
by a graceful force, having scaled any upheavals.

**Yirra**

Like a mouth in the iron-ore earth
the rock-shelter whispers

through fragments of bone, through charcoal
and tools of stone.

Not far from Paraburdoo, a desert town
or the mining contours of Mt Whaleback.

Through the last glacial age, through dry heat
through fifty thousand years

voices whisper.

## Minyirr Park, Broome


In Minyirr Park behind the dunes, an easterly
      subdues the rolling spinifex. I picture you walking
         among the wheaten shades of sand cover


      the path an amber ribbon meandering
for miles by semi-arid leaves. You stop
      before clusters of auburn pods, eye-catching


        as earrings in the face of acacia's green
      and two finches (double-barred), searching
in lavender pea flowers. So much to awe you:


  lizards scurrying, a flicker of wings
      the white of ghost gums and over the rise
the turquoise sea, curling at its edge.

## To Speak of Grasses

1

From the back paddocks of my mind
I look to the base of each rise   each mesa   each range
grass mounds huddled over the ground

like sentinels bowing   side by side
in their Pilbara meandering
their matting profuse.

They don't speak of lack or loss
these home-spun hummock grasses grow the land
in humble knots   there:

in a dry ravine bedded by light-scrubbed river red gums
skirting each mulga   feathery or lobed   with resin or none
stitching the black of a cool burn in monotone.

They speak of impermanence
and the certainty
of termites and lizards for goshawks.

Outside our tent   a dingo
slinks by snappy gums   coarse-barked mallees
and grasses fringing the red sand.

2
So many hidden in morning light at Murujuga:
only a few outlines on the fine-grained boulders heaped
on each other— a huge emu and a ship present themselves.

It is enough to know the significance of these signs
on the russet-brown rocks.

We walk low-voiced among the creamy abundance
of desert bloodwoods    by a midden of shells among grasses
and Sturt's desert pea    blazing in blood-red & black.


3
In Joffre Gorge    facing blocks jutting out—
home to rock figs and grasses in crevices.

A few scramblers come then leave
having tested themselves on narrow shelves.

A man wades upstream to look down the length
of the watercourse    soaking his jeans and shoes.

It's hard to process the time taken
to gouge shapes    to foster life.

No water flows over the fall
        but in the deep green pool
  the rock meets its own.

## From the Cheese Tree

*Glochidion ferdinandi*


It took me a while to clean the heap of heart
shapes from their whorls—an hour of nimble
fingers, easy thoughts—to separate each nub

of new bio-code from its hold. To see them
so red, so plump, these flesh-veiled nuggets
ready for sowing, to re-figure bared clay

or sandy soil on the country's eastern rim. Rich
and promising like the flowerings from Emily
her dump dot creations from the centre.

Young seeds, dispatched too early by rainbow
parrots, lay in a buff haze over the ground.
Apart from birds, I disturbed a few moths

one pale spider and three larvae. I don't know
what could've been more fruitful, than reaching
for those branches to harvest their seeds.

## Suspended

Sixty metres below me, there's nothing
to see through the viscous blue, then

you come into view. The wide smile
of your idle mouth, your spotted hide.

You push silently ahead, your gill flaps
opening and closing clam-tight, your tail

sweeping this way and that. I'm finning
fast but I can't keep up with you whale shark

my fortune great as these unfathomable
depths, my quick delight, my delirium

my breath suspended as you take yours.

**In the Glare on Shell Beach**


On the turquoise-blessed west coast
lies a sandless beach for the crunch
under feet, for the sieve of childlike

hands: cockles, heaped for kilometres
metres deep in places we're told
each as small as a young thumb.

Cockles, once alive in the hyper-saline
water, algae-powered, algae-buffered.

Nearby, a quarry for coquina
the soft stone from compacted shells
cut into blocks to build The Old Pearler.

Nearby, crammed with memorabilia
from 1884, in bakelite-black and grey
the Hamelin Pool Telegraph Station.

But we're on the dunes, searching
for a whole bivalve among the dazzle.

## Antidote

Sun in a halo of cloud, sky a riffraff of high
uncertain shapes, some breaking away

troubling the land across the lake.
The stark glint on windows near the water.

Thornbills zip around an old grey gum.
Wind thrums with cool, moist scent—last night's

rain flows a stream of bubbles over the path.
You think, how lucky to be here.

Whipbirds, honeyeaters and ravens
drum up a tin-pot band—the show flares

with sulphur-crested cockatoos before
the next sudden shower. People you pass

seem open and warm; your own shortcomings
stowed aside. Three butterflies lift their wings.

And before you hear today's news of suffering
and black hope, of conflict and stormy fraud

you stand stilled as light turns leaves
                    into ripples of shimmer.

## The Old Sand Mining Site

      Come into the nursery. Let your eyes reach
the canopies and linger on the canvas of lines and shades.
      How light paints the leaf-shifting spaces.

Blue wrens loiter by *Westringia.*
      They sketch a path through common couch
and *Commelina.* Nearby wetlands harbour a wash

      of bulrush. There's music in the undulations
of black cockatoos lumbering away.
      A burst of scent as we pass mint bush.

Midgen- and apple berries tempt
      but today we'll collect their seeds
and cuttings from *Correa* and native juniper.

      To bend, to tend to the garden and nursery
is to feel the weight of your shadow-self evaporate
      as if being in no time. Imagine the years

readying for bush renewal or urban
      the stories in everything endemic
from the ground up. This is a place for the heart

      head and hands, they tell me. Belonging thrives
here, lively as a fantail at the bird bath. Come
      among the birdsong and bonhomie with those

sowing or pricking out for stock. And sometime
        take your time to wander in the large shade house
on this old sand mining site off Kalaroo Road

        to stop before the rows and rows of young greenery:
their hues, their habits, their dazzling vigour.

## Buoyant and Slender

after Lucinda Leveille's *Butterfly Flowers in Rose*


We met in the Blue Mountains, having kept
in touch loosely since our time in research
five decades ago. You retired early for your health.


    This gift from you—sweeps me about like the lie
    of the flowers on the paper—the lines buoyant


    and slender, the layering of watercolour
    and texture: deft, light and luxurious.


You brushed it off as a hobby, but it's a window
on the delicacy of your doings for others
and with them, on your downplay of demands


even ageing. On the poise and courage
        you draw from, beyond the present.

## We Saw Him

surface    the curve of his unmarked back
his buff hide coursing with the current.

I imagined him sweeping down to the strands
of strap weed or other underwater grasses:
paddle-and pipe-weed    sea-nymph    wrack
and wireweed holding fast to the sea floor.

There with his dugong snout to nuzzle rhizomes
or forage the sea-meadow    home to those
that scuttle or scramble or swim in their nursery
plot.    Again and again he'd come and go.

We craned from the boat in Shark Bay    looking
for anything: paddle-flippers    dolphin-like-tail.

## Salt Water Streaming

That hard flick of fin saying I'm too close.
The body-shudder, the slick accelerations
of bream, mullet and luderick around me.
Water like silk folding over and over my skin.

In morning light, each fingerling's lateral line
shines yellow above a band of turquoise.
They fly past in their cluster, too many to count.

A diamond-fish leaves a dozen of her moon-
shaped kin circling a corner pole in the baths
of Belmont. She nibbles fuzz on a floating strand
of *Posidonia.* Then another and another.

To be with these breath-taking beings
my strokes unskilled, our common ancestor
long gone. Yet now a southerly's whipping

the lake, with no fish in view, nor the seagrass.
When the blur clears, fish will fin brightly
in and out of the netted holes in their haven.

## East Beacons

On the Muogamarra track we passed
      people with cameras on a golden whistler
      and any number of shrubs billowing
with colour and the bearing of bees.

The display centre named plants.
      I knew I'd forget the Latin or Greek
      but not how time disappeared as we walked.
We needed nothing more.

You stopped to examine the shoots
      on a burnt-out trunk, and berries
      high in the pine-leaved geebung
among an over-flowering of pink.

I took photos, though not enough
      of the glory peas, their yellow petals
      like beacons. The Hawkesbury lay
in the sure blue of the sky. Calm as faith.

## Blue Blood

Released, it slid from the clear container
held for close viewing, along with
the pipe fish, shrimp and seahorse
I'd netted from the lake's eel grass.

Its arms aligned snug
behind its fleshy head and mantel, electric
blue rings flashing. It was small enough
to fit in my palm, vulnerable as a baby

but for the toxin in its bite.
I felt I was standing at the edge
of creation, before the lively priming
of ions into the first simple mix

of molecules, setting evolution
cleverly in motion. To form a creature
such as the octopus, king of the boneless
beings, an astute survivor. My heart

reached for it, copper blood coursing
through its chambers. I watched it propel
itself through the water, then disappear
quickly under a brown leaf on the sand.

## A Matter of Fact on Yardie Creek


We could be there now: the osprey stilled
her eyes fixed on us from an eyrie of tousled

sticks above the boat. Rock wallabies leap
about stone marbled in gradients of charred

orange, ash-grey and white.
Fig roots trail from the cliff—each plumbline

stopping short of the green briny water
where mullet graze. You're beside me

but we don't speak
            the panorama too big for us.

## Bleached, Bountiful

*It is strange, Australians love the sea,*
*but most of us are blind to what's in it.*
Isobel Bennett AO, 1909-2008


Isobel typed a letter to Dr. Francois
Director of Fisheries, on how the platforms
and waters around the Solitary Islands
would make *a magnificent marine park*

since thirty-four species of coral live
south of the Great Barrier Reef, since rock
pools teem with anemones, sea urchins
and colonies of tube-building worms.

At Minnie Water, the beach is covered
in shells of all sizes, in segments of spirals
and cones and smoothed pieces piled up:
bleached, bountiful     and protected.

**Sea Web**

A bank of cloud leaden as slate, yet curled
        at its edge with a lip of marbled jade.
On sand darkened by rain, six men net
        a shoal they'd watched earlier.

Like fish I'd seen through my mask:
        their skins lively with bronze and silver
a luminous wildness above the pinks and purples
        shaped as *Mollusca* couched on rock.

This hauling of fish for the plate, common
        and certain as the shifting of substance
to feed other life, cell by cell. The living debt.
        As even opaque eggs bundled in blades

of amber kelp join an undersea food web.
        The rain paused; waves whitened rocks.
As the sky broke within a fan of light, fish
        floundered in the grey tray of the truck.

**Into the Froth**

*for Lyla*


Two dozen nippers vault over waves on their boards
to the buoy, arms pulling, legs flailing, splashing like motors.


They churn the blue in a continuous current
another hundred metres along at Blackies Beach


turn and paddle back to shore. Twice each week
in the season they train, learning to read the surging


collapsing sea at its edge, its tides and rips for safety.
Volunteers urge them on, standing in orange vests


among the young chests striving past in pink.
We huddle on the beach against the southerly.


They'll meet for contest each Sunday as if at early
morning church, families congregating on the fringe.


At the end of this hour, I'm exhausted for them, but
they drop their boards and run back into the froth.

# In the Company of Lovers

**Their Presence**

Straight away you're taller, sprung firm
by their ecstatic vocal runs and upscaling

by their light-tripping over pages of dogma
in this opening chorus of the *Magnificat.*

To hear such voices rise above the swaying
strings and airs of blown breath, continuo

and drum strike. To hear the swell to ear-
tingling fortissimo, undistorted, unpropelled

by any e-device or structure, other than
the clever acoustic leaves below the ceiling

and above the rippled wooden walls
in the filled Concert Hall. To hear such clarity.

Stationed on the stage in black
the full spectrum of tones, distilled from

years of practice, years of learning, brims
from the fibres and folds of their registers

as from the depths of their diaphragms
                    they sing out clear joy.

## The Long Sequel

*for Ian*


1

Tiffs bubble up like hot-spots in super-heated
soup. Though now our brains light up more
in the let-it-be circuitry. Tonight, sharing
a snapper, we search for flesh and memories:

the chef carving for our wedding guests
in the revamped suburban hotel, names
we barely recall, my mother meeting yours
awkward speeches, how little we knew.


2

When I said palms swaying in the air
were like sounds to a score of music you said
*listen.* I was hearing Vivaldi for the first time
thinking this is how music should be, seasons

rolling in with the fronds arcing out each
theme, each fine strand pacing from the last
like notes, and you, my new-found friend
your eyes were closed, your body stilled.


3

The moon throws wafers of white over
the land's pale canvas. Frost hardens.
Inside, our young child reaches for the cat
wakening slowly as Orion falls from the sky.

4

I see you gardening by the dogwood
its flowers a profusion of upturned hands
like the decades of demands of a family
of five. Cat sits close by; a wattle bird

complains. There's a surfeit to juggle: egos
agendas, jobs, study, exams, sickness, sport
chores; motion like the erratic movement
of molecules on the go, too fast at times.


5

I can hold this relic of bluestone and bring
to mind our sojourn in Kingfisher country. She-
oaks drooped into back pools; rapids washed
past. We canoed above eels, a solitary turtle.

Water gums bent under the business of bees.
We swam, we slept, wrapped in river zest
cleansed of doubt, focussed by the river's
force, cocooned in the river's light.


6

Tonight, I'm beyond happy. Our three
and theirs will be with us in our home.
Songs ring in my head; food and house
prepared; even the rain that's fallen

for days can't dampen my spirits.
A spread of wattle gathered this morning
is a sunny welcome on the kitchen bench.
They'll be here soon.


7

The bush is lighter now with new leaves
in young green. *Zieria* is covered all over
by a mist of pale flowering. *Clematis* drapes
wherever it can. This has happened quickly

like the fifty years of knowing you
your eye for design, ear for notes, hands
for love. The flowers from you are similar
to those I held then, your skin still a thrill.

# One Night in November

We were listening to Schubert's *Fantasie*
for four hands    You recognised the key

such a gift I thought    I don't recall details
of our meal    though our minds were free

to relish the flavours of conversing
The night was heady as the scent

of honey-myrtle    light as leaves in mid-air
we slow-spiralled down

each to our own realm
the earth too    holding us

**In the Company of Lovers**
after Beethoven's *Triple Concerto*

She leans back at the end of the bar
flourishes her bow with a wide arc
    into the void, settling you in this new

world, two centuries old. His furrowed
    brow, her pursed lipstick-red lips. She
turns briefly to scan the others on stage

    as B flips the page, his hands taut
a shepherd conducting his fine flock
    in Berlin. Here there's no aggressor

at a country's border, no sudden fire
    nor crime scene; they're shaping sound
sweeping you up in the lilt and pulse

    setting you among trees, each
a note of acclaim in the company
    of lovers, giving these harmonies

their purpose, attentive as the bird
    beneath the heart-shaped leaves
of the native poplar, *Homalanthus.*

    M lifts his brow, his face perspiring.
Others quiver in time with the score.
    If only Beethoven could hear today's

tears in the largo, grief pouring
    from the cello; the piano and violin musing
on tenderness late in the quiet

    light of a new moon without birdsong
the stars driving you into your own ether.
    You're in the company of lovers giving

wholly as they know how. Your feet tap
    and take you for a spin, you're wrapped
in the quickening pace, away from angst.

    The end comes fast. Bold
as the glare of a summer sunrise
    the notes soar into your mind's sky.

## As the Audience Rises

She enters in a shock of pink and shimmer—
shoes matching her full-length strapless gown.
She raises the violin, her eyes close, brows lift.

We're in the front row, the hall full. Applause
bursts after each score: *The Long Goodbye*
*The Leopard, Paper Planes, Hedwig's Theme.*

In the encore, the man behind me stops
coughing, but just as all on stage are deep
in the final tender bars of *Schindler's List*

clapping and cheering erupt.
Her eyes flash.    Her jaw drops.

Now there's no chance of leading all of us
to that ethereal place of exquisite quiet
to idle in    like a long exhale after an excess.

She turns with the conductor. They bow low.

## Before the Border

after Rosalie Gascoigne's *Feathered Fence* (1978-79)


No swans nor cows nor sheep graze:
five fences submerge half-way across
in water pale and calm as the underside
of pearly clouds. Thousands of feathers

lay here years ago, a midden of moulting
in the southern marshes, as if waiting
for Rosalie to gather, clean and tether
their float across the gallery floor.

White plumes from swan underwings
feather affection for this lake
its footprint now close to the highway.
This old friend floods us with history:

the way nearby ranges channel its level
to rise without river or sea and empty
over grass. It's the entrance to our past
in the capital, our children's cradle

a valley by mountains and bush. Small
birds glide about reeds and a patch
of algal pink at the water's edge. Inside
the car, an old song hums a lilting cadence

to the rumble of tyres drumming the road.
When we're up on the ridge, we'll look out
for the quiet show of old grass trees before
the border and the tempo of city buildings.

## About a Year

i

Her owl eyes, her tongue rolled ready
for her mother's breast even as she tries

at six weeks to guide her fingers to meet
a lilac ribbon, murmuring all the while.

Gazelle-like, her sister skips over sand
and races into shallow water, kicking it

into diamonds, pausing to watch the surge
come closer, till it runs over her legs

with the suck and pull and re-swelling
about her. She drops, wanting froth

to swamp her chest and propel her
as if she could swim. Then bolts

beyond the tide, turns willy-nilly
spikes the waves with giddy shrieks.

ii

Those weekdays, my time was not my own
my mind awash with constant chatter.

I'm in the company now of lizard trails
and flannel flowers, the heath giving up

its secrets this Saturday in September
the sky filling with birdcalls about coastal

wattles making seed, and eager young
geebungs in backlit green on the sand.


iii
She bends like a rag doll to reach the teether
she'll bring to her lips and into her mouth.

She breaks from her mother's breast to fix
on her sister. But most of all she likes to settle

on a rug and look into the lullaby of leaves
in the breeze, her gaze unbroken.

Her sister calls to the moon as if to a friend.
*Hmm,* she says; *how do I get it?* her face

to the grass, her fingers on her porcelain
chin, a pose striking as Rodin's sculpture.

*I want to hold it and bring it here.*
                    *I need a ladder.*


iv
At play with the three-year-old, I'm Pip
to her Posy, the ogre's wife to her Jack.

I'm the steward in her plane, customer
in her café, patient in her surgery

traveller on her train. And when we race
I'm the chaser and the chased.


v
The Watagans brood in deep blue.
The wind is icy. Only one swallow


graces the grass under a broken slab
of cloud. I know again to dart from game


to game, to hunger for story.
And I'm drawn to ask why


I'd want more time to myself
why I'd want less of the bluster


and pace of grandchild-filled days.
My eyes brim with her longing


to touch a magpie, a galah's breast
the yellow crest of a cockatoo


and to roll down the long slope of grass
to where those birds stooped to forage.


vi
Nine months old, her fingers eager
for berries, roasted veggies, lean meat.


No teeth, no allergies so far, not even
prawns my father couldn't eat.

We move from room to room, my finger
gripped by her left hand. She shakes

what she holds, drops it and watches
but is stilled more by the acts of birds.

She's dauntless with her sister's antics:
that sudden squeeze of too much love

sudden grab and toss of her toy. Yet
when her sister twirls to 'I Like to Move It'

she nods her head, flails her arms, and
squeals like a whistling kettle on the boil.

vii
This week they'll begin in daycare
good for them, I tell myself, but argue.

Hard to accept change, up high
near the register where tears flow.

viii
There's no escaping the freshness
of air brushed by eucalyptus leaves

flushed by low cloud from this heavy-wooded
land beyond the swamp lilies and gully of ferns.

Nor would I want to, the scent bringing
with it a portal to where the birds glide over

the understory of *Breynia* and *Dodonea*
and about the hundreds of trunks:

straight or multi-stemmed, tannin-stained
flecked or peeling in a sclerophyll harmony

of slow rhythms by the leaf-strewn track.

## Ballast

after Davida Allen's *The Walk in Bush,* 2018


The poinciana shades like a hand spread
        suspended in hallowed air. Perhaps

this is a place to weather any fear, the bush
        coming in close around you, breaths

mingling among the new tips and buds
        and a fantail's call above lines of light.

You're drawn to this painting of two: their hats
        the same shape and scarlet, their hands

in an easy union; the elder's face is brushed
        with mishap and fortune, the child's

in unabashed strokes of freshness. A ballast
        for difficult days—as if to say there's

refuge in a hand or this hillside laden with trees
        sunlight and shadows painting their trunks.

**In These Few Hours**


       A pinwheel of catapulted energy, she's
              a tussock rolling over the windless lawn
her nine-year-old body on the move.


How her younger cousin tries, upending
          herself into keen shapes in mimicry over
the hours. The youngest    all toes


       on the grass as if on moss.
Inside, she pulls handles, her fingers plump
             in my old hands. When she raises her leg


to climb as if nothing will stop her
        I remember how I'm ageing fast
the loss of go seems exponential.


       I try to translate her sounds. She repeats
            each till I get it right as if she's older
than her year. She cries for her mother.


Outside, there's war and greed
         the hungry and homeless, the curdling
of our planet. Work pressing in on me


       before—to balance life's ledger
         leave a legacy—has no traction now as I lift
her warm, nuggety body to roll around

on the bed, laughing at distraction.

    When they leave, I find crusts and half-chewed
cheese over the kitchen bench, but in their scrap books

   I see the lemon myrtle leaves
     from our walk, splashed with bold colours
bright as their starburst selves.

# Gaze

after Laura Jones' *Arcadia*, 2020


Like the splash and dash
of windblown petals


freefalling


past sasanquas over-
flowing from a basket, past the hive
in a lotus pod, leaves large as plates


past the bole of a bloodwood
the spread on *pauciflora* in late summer
the figured greens of a phasmid


Because nothing unravels you
like the face flowering your mind

## Impromptu

*our place in the connectedness of things*
       Gail Hennessy, *'Our Eclectic Garden'.*


His hands skip over the piano keys
  trilling them as if there's no weight
in the years we've been together


in rhythms of family and garden
  by a backdrop of native bush. He sets
the harmony with chords melodic


as the orchids and roses in their seasons.
  He improvises variations: lunch
by the lillypilly, lorikeets in the grevilleas


and birdbath, a grandchild running
  across the lawn by bromeliads and ferns
that haven for magpies in the heat.


There's a familiar cadence, welcome
  as a homecoming. Lucky to have such
company, lemon and lavender, *ficifolia*


and cycad, memories from our mothers'
  gardens in the *breynia* and *feijoa.*
Shape and size and colour are songs


to save us. At the end of his impromptu
  the room overflows with the slow
luscious notes of gardenias.

## Again

*for June*


She sits motionless on my lap, eyes fixed, ready
for the double-page-spread in icy blue when she'll leap up

shouting *OH NO*, in tune with the only words shown
as the penguin, hindered by a seal, is blocked

in her bid to feed her chick. The birds' eyes are drawn
large as wheels as if watching us as the story unrolls

yet I'm in the learner's seat, seeing this two-year-old
rapt in the mother's mind-set to face trouble, even

if it takes pages before the chick gets fed, before it asks
for more. After I read to her five times, she says    *Again.*

## Unwavering

*for Etta*


We walked beside a grey gum, its fruit
by the path. I shook seeds fine as dust
into my palm saying, one of these

could make one of those. I watched
as she lifted her eyes from the ground up
past the untidy bark, leaves dangling

branches angling out. Up to the top
she went with her three-year-old eyes
of surprise in the unwavering light.

## Snapshot

*for Macy*


That pink splash across the page: her first drawing
I've kept for years for its oversized head-in-body-


figure with lines straight up as hair, out for hands
and legs, the face of circles within. I gathered


her paper trail of dresses, dream homes, people
in her stories. The cast of Harry Potter, Taylor Swift


her own fiction. There's the one of her floating
facing the shoreline before a great spiralling wave


her surfboard nearby. That source of confidence.
She found her voice early, singing in the pram.


Sang a solo at the interview to begin school.
Now she's teaching her younger sister the moves


from the rehearsal, their differences swept away
energy racing as she sings *Rolling in the Deep.*

# Walking Each Other

## News in the Wind

*for Jean*


To go with you to Crackenback
              and back to Dead Horse Gap
seeing over slopes and colours close to the earth
                purple eyebright up among snow daisies.


          We'd make our way to the river's white-water
thrashing at decibels, buoying renewal
         in gums, mint bush, alpine pepper, and us
              not wanting to move, fixed on the scene.


We'd take the whole day and then another to wander.
         About our feet, there'd be ribbony grass
                felted buttercups, a surplus of billy buttons.
Nothing but good news in the cold wind.

## Chelmer Continuo

Standing at the river's weedy edge
    I'd hear the bird, persistent in the pastels

of a cloudy dawn. I'd walk home past high-set
    houses, their paint rippling in the sun; turn

into the avenue with bay figs and laurels
    reaching across the road.

***

With our children we saw boats
    on grassy banks, homes restumped

restored, restyled—verandahs rising
    above the aroma of *Brunfelsia.*

We heard the koel call across the river.

***

As if rewinding a tape, the machine
    out-dated, the past a long way back.

**Exotic**

Camphor laurel, *Cinnamomum camphora*


They swell the hills to the distant ocean
with their evergreen spheres. Foreign
and invasive, but 'something happens

when you look into them', my aunt said.
One fended the entrance to her garden.
Young then, I'd take the train to her home.

We'd go inside for tea and simple cake.
The children's clothes she sewed—her skill
her flair—hung readied in the dining room.

Driving now, I wish she could see them
in the silvering breeze, leaves edging
the scene with waves of abundant lace.

## Tarnished Youth

She asked me to put the kettle on.
I hopped up, grabbed the generous

arc over its copper-shine body, lit
the gas. The noise was a wheeze

I stayed to hear. The breeze increased
and a magnificent apple-green flame

I'd never seen, shot from the spout
and flickered. It was a colour I wanted

to wear in crisp light cotton, to counter
the heat of our long humid summers.

Suddenly the spout fell off.
What? I thought and stopped the gas.

I lifted the lid and saw I'd failed
to check on the water inside.

There was none. Her keepsake
kettle was done for. And so was I.

## Looking On

I'd walk through the foyer
            of the Florey
left into the hallway
left into the second lab
            its windows
onto van Gogh yellows
my steps keen
            for the assays
the bio-procedures
following truth    in facts
            the place abuzz
with lively purpose
novel as the seasons
            out of Brisbane
my first work    at twenty
two elms looking on.

# Dancing

Picture the slow trickle of fluid
      through the deep earth, settling
in a seam or vein or node

      over millennia, shifting into spheres
in sandstone in the Great Artesian Basin
      before birds feathered the skies.

At White Cliffs, miners hand-pick
      for potch in the stone. How light
plays about the silica-rich shapes.

      She wore the opal in a band
of gold. In the living room listening to Bach
      she'd work her crafts, two cats

nearby. In her paddock near the Grampians
      we scattered her ashes
a grandniece dancing the Highland Fling.

      Turning the gem of her ring
I catch a flush of scarlet rose, a patch
      of Pacific blue, a dash of eye-green.

# The Pond

after Valerie Marshall Strong Olsen

If I had an artist's eye
and will to sit   I'd watch
the pond daily   paint it
a dozen times as she did
at dusk   in rain   at noon
with bells   in summer   in
half-light. I'd know how
to handle any tones   any
illusions of substance and
where to draw the line

**Reminder**

after Arthur Boyd's *The Beach* (1944)


My father lists his medicines for the doctor
        his letters sliding into each other.


Tubing of good air glides with him
        long enough to reach the porch in the sun.


Small-framed, blond hair like Arthur's
        same age too, though Dad doesn't speak


of his war-time in New Guinea. Nor
        would he focus on Arthur's canvas:


the figure in a coffin-boat, a parched god
        beneath a troubled sun, those menaced


hands. War blasts our screens every night.
        Back then they handed recruits cigarettes.


*Remind the kids* (his breath laboured) *never to smoke.*
        On the way to the doctor, the driver calls him *Digger.*

## A Certain Age

Legally blind, her hearing so low she slept
through the shrill of her smoke alarm

that woke neighbours. Malpractice in surgery
gave her a stoma bag. Then the fluttering

in the upper chambers of her heart.
How would they find her filmy veins each day?

How would she cut the pills precisely?
My mother spoke often of her mother: up early

in the bakery, hands folding butter into flour
on the marble slab. Baking gave her such joy too.

I recall the food she made to welcome
us from school:   fine pastries   cakes like air.

## Always Flying

after the film *Fire on the Water* at Denham WA
which used Arvo Pärt's *Fratres*


In 1941, two ships off Shark Bay: the HMAS *Sydney*
draws close before the merchant ship's trick:


reflagging & guns firing from the HSK *Kormoran.*
Shrill sounds of a violin heighten the flames


on the screen: the cruiser's turrets destroyed
guns down, officers lost. Piano discord notes


the moonless night, then soothes for the sinking
of the boats.      Seven hundred and twenty-six


now lie on the sea bed.      Honoured too
in Carnarvon by the walk beside the river.


Outside in Geraldton silver gulls shape a dome
of remembrance, their soldered wings always flying.

## To the Edge

after Robert Juniper's *On the Gibb River Road*


He takes no notes, makes no sketches

                                        rolls memory like a Kimberley pearl

                      sets his eyes on the slim lines of freshwater crocs


the tubs of boabs                  screw pines by Bell Gorge


Termite mounds are triangles in ochre        dryandras spike

        white dragon flowers     spinnaker    over a skeletal soil

           His mind figures

                  with the shapes and tones of heat and loss


        even *Kingia*   that southern grass-tree look-alike

                  clusters and curls against the sky

## The Vase

The sea painted almost as it was:
        placid swell, no rip, the turquoise
tide before the year's first full moon.


        It's difficult to find words
to define attraction—a voice mesmeric
        as drops of silver mercury rolling
their sheen around, each holding


        its own till they coalesce. Grey
grains swirl in the foreshore on the vase
        from you, bringing back that swim:


floating before the sun-lit kelp
        sea urchins about pink algae
watching the eyes of a dozen squid
        passing under the yellow-tails.


And you on the sand        waiting.

**Breathing Homes**

A strangler fig is leaning    sixty metres up.
        You say it'll fall soon    but what do either of us really know.
            Everything here is oversized.


Roots wrap each other    vines snake about Gondwanan trunks
                    a flourish of ferns high in trees    spill out
to celebrate the sun.


            It's dark underfoot and damp.    Yet on the side
        of the slope is the misty blue of another range
                    seemingly close    a trick to fall
for    metres down and metres up    bound by mountains


        and their verdure.    The thunder of Tristania Falls
                saturates my bones    cinnamon scent
                from *Doryphora sassafras* reminds me of language
I want to learn.    I think of the world within


            each plant    the way photons of light unlock
cellular strands out of sight    to bring the seasonal brilliance
                    before us    the breathing homes


for birds and others to make their own


                                    while we walk
beneath the fluted notes of a grey shrike-thrush.

## Vaudeville

1

Two males in close    each breast gilded
each head and tail dotted white    a light
streak on the brow    red flash of rump
Pardalotes in a fuss of feathers
unbinding time among forest vines


2

Lyre-mouth of many calls
clever twister of the news
clear                 persistent

listen to me    listen to me
Black    beady    urgent-eyed
metres up the peppermint


3

Look at you    harlequin bird    eating
my candy-pink grevilleas    stamens drifting
from your beak as you splice your way
through each bloom    pacing up the stem

overbalancing nearly yet never    You've
taken three down already    take all the time
in your world with your gold    black    green
your bold red    your white cheeks

When you leave    I'll prune the bush
to foster more flowers and cluster more
early mornings with kinetic colour

# Headache Vine

*Clematis glycinoides*


a doona trailing over *Pittosporum*
whales' bones laid out


a sphere over a young sapling
that wave just arrived at the shoreline


a slide down a river of green
she's a siren languishing


luminescence stringing the foreshore
an old clothes line between trunks


white dabs of erasure fluid
a tepee in a red gum sapling


bridal veil flowing over an embankment
a flag at half-mast


all that paper spilled out of a bin
the garlanded reins of a horse pulled taut


*Clematis* starring in Green Point Reserve
muffling spring

## High Spirits

We caught Kosciusko at sunrise & moonset
        the sky in its ten-minute flush to full sun.
Ranges around sharpened to icy blue. Ravens

keen as guards, stood by patches of snow
        stained pink. Blooms among grasses cloaked
the hills, a vista distilled to the colours of ease

where life befriends death. We came across
        small-leafed heaths and herbs, surviving even
when wind blasts the year's forbidding cover.

Later, you sat out of the westerly, your back
        to the cairn. Two bogongs brushed my face
as a fluster of moths flickered about us.

## November

i
Cream canopies on the hills and wetlands frame
the train's window–my reading now derailed
by this carpet mid-way to the sky.

After the Hawkesbury, the train rattles past
flashes of flame trees, clouds of lilac, burnished
silky oaks: their stories swelling the day's spell.

ii
Maybe it's the stature of a yellow box or the way
bark ripples down its trunk or the white pouring
of its pollen. Maybe it's the honey-scent-warmth
of the spring day that stops me on this hillside.

So much happening. Snow falling in Yosemite
new demands threatening world leaders.
But to be near a *melliodora*—
it surfaces again: that settling of self.

iii
Driving the Putty Road under the gleam of black
wattles, hills going straight up to caves in grey stone.
Shadows hold the secrets of Wollemi and Yengo.

We're among the rugged and raw, all senses sharp.
Words fall short in this place of possibility.
How can we ever know who, what lives here

though we flushed out red-browed finches
by a road-side fire-place near a sandpaper fig
the air warm and close as a cloak.

## Walking Each Other

*i.m. Jill McKeowen*


I'm calling for those who can't navigate
    the narrow-rugged path, the muddy patches
or sandstone steps by Popes Glen Creek.


Those who'd never find themselves walking
    into minted air from *piperita* in the morning
or see the ferns massed and mellow


about the low run of water, or the ridge
    of blue mountain ash near the cliff's hanging
garden. Those who'd not hear the spinebill


staccato above the creek's flailing
    from so much rain, or the close chatter
of crimson lorikeets. How waratah reds crown


this country. In town there's an abundance
    of rhododendrons and a flood of buttercups
straining out of the flats. But now I'm calling


from the pool of Boyd Beach
    up the two hundred and seventy-eight steps
to Glen Phillips Lookout and the trail


of understorey smoke bush, that welcome
    to the plateau. Now sunshine wattle is set
with seed and fog has bedded itself below.

Two black cockatoos skim
    the bed, they're slipping in and out
making waves as they cross Grose Valley.

And they answer me, my virtual company:
    *we're walking each other.*
    *Wherever we are. And whenever.*

## The Mooring

after Michèle Heibel's *Follow the Line* (2023)


There was always washing waiting on the line
Often a sweep of silver gulls about the harbour
of trees    Ever the slip of her young hand in yours

Enough to hold onto    Moments like pinpricks
of light from the old home    shimmering
You recall her simple words    Her joy

on the boat    Her childish vim    Determined
ways    You gave her all your time
Shaped her    And she you

It was a gift
        a mooring against these later years
                        You unfurl the sail

## Marching Still

after The People's Climate March, New York City, 21 September 2014


Two minutes silence before the siren, thunderous
as a sonic boom when it reached the group wearing
white lab coats on 86th street. I stood next to Joan


a special needs teacher from Long Island, the crowd
dense, heat rising, both of us with sore feet.


Before crossing Central Park, I passed a guitarist
playing *A Day in the Life of a Fool* while squirrels
bounded about red berries on Downy Hawthorns.


When someone raised a sign about *The Debate*
we yelled is *over.*     *Over*     again and again.


Back home I hear those voices
throughout droughts, mega-fires and floods.


We're marching still.


Shouting still.

# Notes

The poem 'Revelations from Dudley' draws on information from Geology of the Newcastle coastline, New South Wales, compiled by Phil Gilmore, 2014. See:
https://geotrailandnaturetours.com.au/

'Yirra' refers to a sacred site in the Pilbara—at Rio Tinto's Eastern Channar mine—which, through excavations, affirms 'the presence of Yinhawangka People in the region for more than 50,000 years'. See:
https://www.yinhawangka.com.au/yirra-study/

For the poem 'To Speak of Grasses' species of *Triodia* and *Plectrachne* commonly referred to as spinifex, are grasses and not to be confused with the coastal *Spinifex.*

In 'From the Cheese Tree', Emily refers to Emily Kam Kngwarray, an Aboriginal artist from the Utopia Community in the Northern Territory. See:
https://en.wikipedia.org/wiki/Emily_Kame_Kngwarreye

'The Old Sand Mining Site' refers to the organisation *Trees in Newcastle*, a nursery for native plants. See:
https://treesinnewcastle.org.au/

The quote in 'Bleached, Bountiful' was taken from the Papers of Isobel Bennett, National Library of Australia MS 9348.

In the poem 'In the Company of Lovers', the music refers to Beethoven's Concerto for Violin, Cello, and Piano in C major, Op. 56 (Triple Concerto) performed by Mutter, Ma, Barenboim and the West Eastern Divan Orchestra: https://music.apple.com/de/album/beethoven-tripleconcerto-visual-album-live-at-philharmonie/1503547758.

'As the Audience Rises' refers to the performance of the music of John Williams by the Sydney Symphony Orchestra conducted by Simone Young, and featuring Anne-Sophie Mutter on violin. This took place on Saturday 11 November 2023 in the Concert Hall of the Sydney Opera House.

Robert Juniper, referenced in 'To the Edge', was an acclaimed Western Australian artist, 'known for his evocative and poetic vision of the Australian landscape, often painted from an aerial perspective'. See: https://www.junipergalleries.com.au/

In the poem 'Looking On', the Florey Building is the name given (in 2015) to the refurbished John Curtin School of Medical Research. I began my working career in 1972 as a Research Assistant to Graeme Laver, a Research Fellow in the School's Department of Microbiology. The laboratory work focussed at that time mainly on the structure of Influenza Virus and the mechanism of its antigenic variation.

## Acknowledgements

I am indebted to Dael Allison, Jenny Blackford and Jean Kent for their poetic expertise and generous reading of and responses to my work. Also, I'd like to thank other members of the Hunter Writers Centre, especially Leonie Wellard, Eve Gray and Julie Simpson who provided valuable feedback on the manuscript. And to Gail Hennessy (now deceased) and Gillian Telford for comments on certain poems. I am grateful too for the suggestions and encouragement from Brenda Proudfoot and Hamilton writer Ruth Cotton.

And most importantly I give thanks for our three: Alicia, Nic and Wil (and their families). And to Ian for love through five decades.

I wish to thank the editors of the anthologies and journals in which the following poems appeared. Some have been revised.

'About a Year', *Verandah* 37, 2022.

'Antidote', *Out of the Shadows* anthology, 2023.

'Before the Border', *Science Write Now*, Edition 9, 2023.

'Blue Blood', Hunter Writers Centre website, 2022. https://hunterwriterscentre.org/

'From the Cheese Tree', *Plumwood Mountain Journal*, Vol 10, Number 1, *The Transformative Now*, 2023.

'In the Company of Lovers', *Poetry of Encounter: The Liquid Amber Anthology*, 2022.

'In the Glare on Shell Beach', as 'In the Glare', *Telling Australia's Truth: Reflections on Australia's past and future*, Ginninderra Press, 2024

'Impromptu' in the Common or Garden Poets conversation, on the Flying Islands Community website.

'Revelations from Dudley', *Science Write Now*, Edition 9, 2023.

'Tarnished Youth', *Science Write Now*, Edition 7.2, 2022.

'The Long Sequel', 2023 ACU Prize for Poetry Anthology, 2023.

'The Old Sand Mining Site' in *Out of the Shadows* anthology, 2023. The poem was awarded second place in the 2022 Alice Sinclair Writing Competition.

'Their Presence', *Griffith Review 81: The Leisure Principle,* 2023.

'Yirra' in Issue Two of *The Marrow,* 2024.

https://www.themarrowpoetry.com/

## About the Author

Born in Brisbane, Kathryn Fry began work as a Research Assistant in Microbiology at the Australian National University, Canberra. Marriage and family intervened in her ten years at the ANU. She gained a Graduate Diploma in Education in 1994 before teaching High School Science for a decade. Following that, she worked at the Australian Bureau of Statistics before retiring and relocating to Belmont NSW with her husband Ian. Her previous books of poetry, both published by Ginninderra Press are: *Green Point Bearings* (2018) and *The Earth Will Outshine Us* (2021).